FOLGER McKINSEY ELEMENTARY SCHOOL

W9-ALV-852

The **St. Lawrence** River

by Tim Cooke

Gareth Stevens Publishing
A WORLD ALMANAC EDUCATION GROUP COMPANY

Please visit our web site at: www.garethstevens.com
For a free color catalog describing Gareth Stevens Publishing's list of high-quality
books and multimedia programs, call 1-800-542-2595 (USA) or 1-800-387-3178
(Canada). Gareth Stevens Publishing's fax: (414) 332-3567.

Library of Congress Cataloging-in-Publication Data

Cooke, Tim (Tim A.).
    The St. Lawrence River / by Tim Cooke.
       p. cm. — (Rivers of North America)
    Includes bibliographical references and index.
    Contents: Linking lakes and oceans—From source to mouth—The life of the river—
Route into Canada—Logs, locks, and lakes—Places to visit—How rivers form.
    ISBN 0-8368-3762-2 (lib. bdg.)
    1. Saint Lawrence River—Juvenile literature. [1. Saint Lawrence River.] I. Saint
Lawrence River. II. Title. III. Series.
F1050.C66   2003
971.4—dc21   2003042744

This North American edition first published in 2004 by
Gareth Stevens Publishing
A World Almanac Education Group Company
330 West Olive Street, Suite 100
Milwaukee, Wisconsin 53212 USA

Original copyright © 2004 The Brown Reference Group plc. This U.S. edition copyright © 2004
by Gareth Stevens, Inc.

Author: Tim Cooke
Editor: Tom Jackson
Consultant: Judy Wheatley Maben, Education Director, Water Education Foundation
Designer: Steve Wilson
Cartographer: Mark Walker
Picture Researcher: Clare Newman
Indexer: Kay Ollerenshaw
Managing Editor: Bridget Giles
Art Director: Dave Goodman

Gareth Stevens Editor: Betsy Rasmussen
Gareth Stevens Designer: Melissa Valuch

Picture Credits: Cover: Boldt Castle, Hart Island, New York. (Skyscan: Jim Wark)
Contents: The Montreal area during winter.

Key: l–left, r–right, t–top, b–bottom.
Ardea: François Gohier 5t, 12b, 13, 27; P. Morris 12t; S. Roberts 24; Corbis: 14; Yann Arthus-Bertrand 10;
Bettmann 18; Bojan Breceli 25; Leonard De Selva 16; David Muench 11t; Richard T. Nowitz 29r; Carl &
Ann Purcell 28; Robert Van Der Hilst 6; Bill Varie 22; Michael S Yamashita 20; Getty Images: 19, 23;
NASA: 8, 29l; Parks Canada: L. Delisle 21r; Still Pictures: Peter Arnold/Jeff Greenberg 21l; Peter
Arnold/Jim Wark 9; Peter Arnold/Alex S. MacLean 26; PhotoDisc: PhotoLink 11b; Sylvia Cordaiy Picture
Library: P. C. Dishart 15; Topham: 17; Travel Ink: Abbie Enock 4/5; Mathieu Lamarre 4l; U.S. Army Corps
of Engineers: Ken Winters 7

Printed in the United States of America

1 2 3 4 5 6 7 8 9 07 06 05 04 03

Table of Contents

Linking Lakes and Oceans

The St. Lawrence River connects the Great Lakes to the Atlantic Ocean. Once known for its fishing grounds and farms, the river is now an important trade route with many cities on its banks.

The St. Lawrence is the largest and most important river in eastern Canada. It flows from Lake Ontario to the Atlantic Ocean. Most of the river runs through Canada, but it also forms part of the northern border of New York state. The river flows through a wide estuary into the Gulf of St. Lawrence, a large inlet of the northwest Atlantic Ocean. The river's estuary and gulf were once filled with wildlife, such as cod and whales. Because of overfishing and pollution in the river, however, some of the wildlife has now disappeared.

River Road

The St. Lawrence River was the main route taken by European settlers heading for the inland of Canada. Many of Canada's major cities stand along its banks, including Quebec and Montreal,

Far right: *A ship passes through one of the many locks along the St. Lawrence Seaway system.*

Below: *A fisherman shows the teeth of a shark caught in the mouth of the St. Lawrence River. The river used to be home to a very large fishing industry.*

The skyline of Montreal stands over the wide St. Lawrence River. This Canadian city stands on a large island in the river and is one of the world's largest river ports.

which were founded by the French as trading posts in the early seventeenth century.

Although it is relatively short, at only 744 miles (1190 kilometers) long, the St. Lawrence River of today is part of a system of canals that links the United States and Canada with ports around the Great Lakes. As such, the St. Lawrence is a vital highway from the interior of North America to the Atlantic coast.

twentieth century, the United States and Canada funded and built new canals and dams and widened channels in existing waterways. The shipping route created is called the St. Lawrence Seaway, and it is one of the world's busiest waterways. Grain from the the Midwest and the Canadian prairies is shipped along the seaway. Coal and iron are other important cargoes, which are taken to factories along the river valley.

The Seaway

After it leaves Lake Ontario, the water in the upper section of the river flows rapidly. These rapids stopped boats from reaching the Great Lakes for many years, until they were bypassed by canals and controlled by dams. In the mid-

1 From Source to Mouth

The St. Lawrence River drains water from the Great Lakes. It flows through a narrow valley between two mountain ranges before flowing into a large gulf on the east coast of Canada.

The St. Lawrence is an ancient river. Its 744-mile (1190-km) course runs through a deep hollow that was formed about six thousand years ago. The hollow runs between the hills of the Canadian Shield—a great rock platform that occupies most of northern Canada—and the northern end of the Appalachian Mountains, which rise in Maine and run south through the eastern United States. About twelve thousand years ago, the hollow was filled with seawater. Over the following six thousand years, however, the seabed rose up, leaving a narrow valley between the mountains. Today, the St. Lawrence runs through this valley.

River Sections

Most of the water in the St. Lawrence comes from the Great Lakes. The five lakes—Superior, Michigan, Huron, Erie, and Ontario—cover an area the size of the state of Wyoming and contain nearly one-fifth of all the world's freshwater.

Below left: *Rock formations loom on the northern bank of the St. Lawrence river near its mouth.*

TRIBUTARIES

- Manicougan
- Ottawa
- Saguenay
- St. Maurice

Lake Nipigon

Thunder Bay

Lake Superior

Duluth

WISCONSIN

Milwaukee

Chicago

The lakes drain an area of about 292,000 square miles (756,000 sq km), mainly from the Canadian province of Ontario. The water flows eastward through short channels from lake to lake and ends up in Lake Ontario. The Niagara River connects Lake Erie with Lake Ontario, and its water has carved the famous Niagara Falls. The water constantly wears away the limestone cliffs over which it flows, so the falls have actually moved upstream about 7 miles (11.2 km) from where European explorers first recorded them as being.

River Sections

The St. Lawrence River flows out of Lake Ontario near the city of Kingston, Ontario, draining almost all of the water from the Great

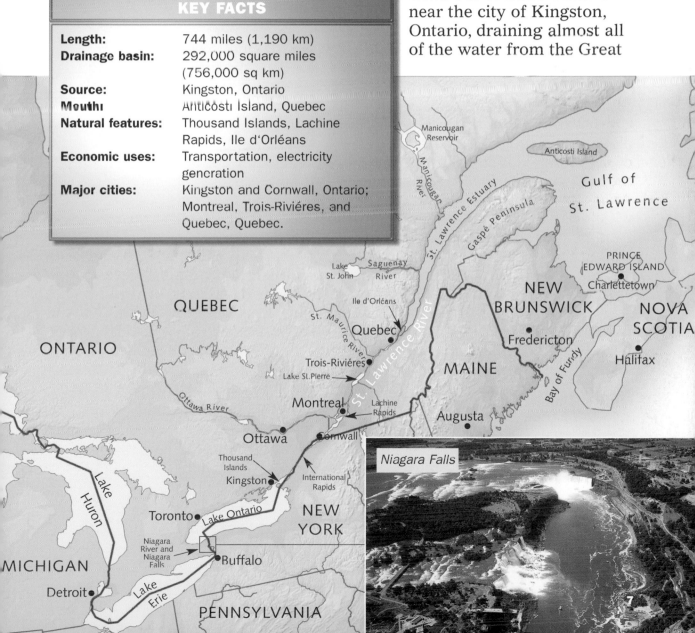

KEY FACTS

Length:	744 miles (1,190 km)
Drainage basin:	292,000 square miles (756,000 sq km)
Source:	Kingston, Ontario
Mouth:	Anticosti Island, Quebec
Natural features:	Thousand Islands, Lachine Rapids, Ile d'Orléans
Economic uses:	Transportation, electricity generation
Major cities:	Kingston and Cornwall, Ontario; Montreal, Trois-Riviéres, and Quebec, Quebec.

Niagara Falls

7

Lakes. Experts divide the river into several sections. The river itself flows from Lake Ontario to Lake St. Pierre, halfway between Montreal and Quebec. North of Lake St. Pierre, the river widens into St. Lawrence Estuary.

Halfway down the estuary, the river's freshwater begins to mix with salty seawater, pushed in and out of the river by the tides. As it flows past Anticosti Island, the St. Lawrence Estuary empties into the Gulf of St. Lawrence, a triangle-shaped inlet.

Lake Ontario to Montreal

After it leaves Lake Ontario, the St. Lawrence River cuts through the rocks of the Canadian Shield. At Thousand Islands, granite outcrops form about seventeen hundred tree-covered islands. The islands are a popular tourist destination. (It was while cruising here that hotel owner George Boldt was said to have invented the famous Thousand Island salad dressing.)

There used to be numerous rapids on the upper section of the river, which falls about 225 feet (69 meters) in only 115 miles (184 km). Near Ogdensburg, New York, is the International Rapids section of the river, where the fast-flowing water forms the border between Canada and the United States.

Below: *Montreal, Quebec, seen from space in winter. West of the city, the St. Lawrence River is frozen solid, while to the east, the water has been kept free of ice so ships can reach the port.*

Most of the river's rapids have been drowned by the lakes created by dams built to control the river's flow. Just south of the city of Montreal lie the Lachine Rapids, which, for many years, were the farthest a boat could travel up the river. Today, they are bypassed by a canal.

To the Gulf

North from Lake St. Pierre, at the beginning of the estuary, the river becomes tidal, which means the level of the river rises and falls twice a day with the tides. However, this far from the ocean, the tide is freshwater pushed upstream by the seawater flowing into the mouth farther downstream.

The river begins to widen rapidly. Between Montreal and Quebec, the river is between 1 mile and 2.5 miles (1.6 and 4 km) wide. It broadens to nearly 90 miles (145 km) across at its mouth.

A number of large islands break up the flow of the river. The 18-mile (29-km) Ile d'Orleans, upstream from Quebec, only became connected to the bank by a bridge in 1935. North of Ile d'Orleans, the freshwater river mingles with saltwater from the Atlantic. Much of the river is often covered by ice during the winter. Reefs of ice cling to the banks of the estuary and chunks of ice flow down the center of the broad river.

In Quebec, the St. Lawrence River meets one of its most important tributaries, the Saguenay River, which flows through a deep gorge originally cut by glaciers. From there, the St. Lawrence deepens very rapidly. At the Saguenay, the river is 80 feet (24 m) deep, but only a few miles downstream, it is more than 1,145 feet (349 m) deep as the river flows into an underwater valley.

Above: *A grand house on one of the Thousand Islands near Alexandra Bay, New York, close to the source of the St. Lawrence.*

2 The Life of the River

The St. Lawrence River is home to an array of wildlife. Whales feed near the river's mouth, countless birds migrate through the area, and untouched wilderness lines much of its banks.

The St. Lawrence River lies roughly between two areas that have different types of plant and animal habitats. To the north of the St. Lawrence River, the weather is cold and icy for most of the year. This land area is covered by conifer forests, with spruce, jack pine, and balsam fir trees. Most of these trees have needlelike leaves that can survive in icy conditions. The trees keep their needles all year-round. Because of this, the trees are

Above: *The Charlevoix Biosphere Reserve in Quebec. Near the river's northern bank is a protected wilderness.*

THE PITCH PINE

The pitch pine is a remarkable conifer tree that grows on both sides of the St. Lawrence River. The trees (left in background) grow to 45 feet (14 m) tall and have a trunk about 3 feet (1 m) in diameter.

Pitch pines have evolved to survive the forest fires that sometimes sweep through the area, either started deliberately by loggers, accidentally by visitors, or naturally by lightning strikes. The pitch pine can not only survive such fires, it needs them to reproduce. The trees' buds sprout new shoots only after the tree is burned in a fire. The pitch pine's cones, which contain its seeds, remain closed for many years. When there is a fire, however, the heat splits the cones, and the seeds are released.

described as evergreen. Conifer forests also grow on the south shore of the river, near its mouth.

The area around the river's source and the region to the south have warmer weather, with longer summers. Forests of broad-leaved trees grow here, including beech, elm, and maple. These trees have flattened leaves, which are shed in the fall and grow again in spring.

Wilderness Area

Although a great many of the conifer trees beside the St. Lawrence have been cut down by loggers, much of

Above: *A snowshoe hare with its white winter coat. The hare's soft fur was once prized by trappers.*

Above: *A young cod swimming near the riverbed. The St. Lawrence Estuary used to be filled with these meaty fish.*

Below: *Fishers in the Gulf of St. Lawrence haul in a net filled with herring, an oily fish eaten all over the world.*

the river's banks are clothed in untouched wilderness. The wildest regions are beside the wide estuary, close to its mouth. Here, the banks are steep cliffs, which make it hard to travel into the forests from the river.

Some areas that are easier to get to (such as the Trois Riviéres, Quebec, region between Montreal and Quebec) have been logged for as long as four hundred years. In the past, some areas of the forest were damaged by logging. Today, the industry is better managed, and measures are taken to ensure that a new tree is planted for every one that is cut down.

River Animals

The largest animals in the area are black bears and moose—the largest type of deer in the world. Smaller animals include weasels, mink, and red foxes. Beavers live in the mountain rivers and streams in the area. They use branches and sticks to build dams across streams to form lakes where they build their lodges. They also feed on the many trees that grow in the area.

European settlers were attracted to the St. Lawrence River for its wildlife. Cod lived in huge shoals, or shallow waters,

THE ENDANGERED BELUGAS

The St. Lawrence Estuary, near its junction with the Saguenay River, is home to a population of beluga, or white whales. Belugas—the name comes from the Russian word for *whitish*—grow to about 15 feet (5 m) long and feed on herring, smelt, shellfish, and squid. Belugas are hunted by killer whales and polar bears. In the past, belugas were also hunted by Native people and Basque whalers, who came from northern Spain and southern France.

The St. Lawrence once had ten thousand belugas living in it. Today, however, that number has fallen to about seven hundred because of hunting and pollution. Beluga hunting was banned in 1978.

in the wide estuary, but centuries of overfishing have made cod rare in the river. Beavers and mink were valuable for their fur. Trappers also reduced the numbers of many furry animals in the forests. Snowshoe hares, which grow white coats in winter in order to blend into the snowy landscape, are now also rare.

The lower reaches of the St. Lawrence River are visited by more than 320 species of birds. Some are inland species, such as the blue jay, the ruffed grouse, and the black-throated warbler. Waterfowl such as goldeneyes, black ducks, and loons spend the winter in the river's reed beds and on sandbanks.

The St. Lawrence is home to both river and sea fish. Salmon, sturgeon, cod, and herring swim in the gulf and estuary. Bass, eels, and perch live in the upper river, but many die from pollution.

Above: *A beluga whale like the ones that live in the river. Belugas are small compared to most types of whales.*

3 Route into Canada

The course of the St. Lawrence shaped modern Canada. It was an important highway into the interior of the continent, and even today, most people in eastern Canada live close to the river.

Before European settlers began to arrive in the sixteenth century, the St. Lawrence region was populated by two main Native groups—the Iroquois and Algonquian people.

Powerful Alliance

South of the river, the Iroquois Confederacy ruled. The Iroquois were an alliance of several peoples from the New England region, including the Mohawk, Oneida, Seneca, Cayuga, and Onondaga.

The Iroquois traded widely with other groups and often allowed other groups into their alliance. They used the land beside the river to grow corn, beans, squashes, and tobacco. They also fished in the river and hunted in the nearby woods. The Iroquois

Below: *French explorer Jacques Cartier leads his men onto the bank of the St. Lawrence River to meet Native people during his search for gold and jewels.*

THE KINGDOM OF SAGUENAY

When Jacques Cartier explored the St. Lawrence River in 1534, the local Iroquois told him stories of an inland kingdom called Saguenay. They claimed that Saguenay was rich with precious jewels and spices. The stories inspired Cartier to locate the kingdom. His first attempt in 1535 failed, but in 1541, Cartier explored the Saguenay River, where he found deposits of what he thought were gold and diamonds. He took his loot back to France, but it turned out his treasure was made up of worthless iron pyrites—fool's gold—and quartz crystals.

lived in wood framed longhouses that were covered in elm bark. Their villages were sometimes protected by rings of wooden fences, called palisades, 15 to 20 feet (4.5 to 6 m) high. Defense was important because there was constant warfare among the many different Iroquois groups and with their Algonquian neighbors.

Northern Neighbors

The Algonquian lived north of the river. They lived in bands of one hundred to three hundred members, which were made up of several family groups. Each Algonquian family had their own lodge, which was made of bent saplings covered with birch bark.

In winter, the Algonquian hunted deer, moose, and other forest animals. They used sleds and snowshoes to move quickly over deep snow. After the snow melted, the Algonquians fished in the river and gathered wild fruits, nuts, and roots. They were expert canoeists and could negotiate all but the largest rapids on the St. Lawrence River.

Above: *A replica of a Native village in the St. Lawrence River area. The settlement is surrounded by a palisade—a tall fence of sharp sticks*

Above: *An illustration of a fur trapper in the woods of Quebec. In the nineteenth century, fur trading was big business in the area.*

of Asia. Cartier did not find the passage, but he did claim the land around the river for the French king, calling it New France.

He made friends with the Iroquois people and sailed up the river as far as the impassable rapids near where Montreal is today. He named the rapids La Chine—China in French—in the hope that China and the rich lands of Asia lay only a little way beyond.

The next important European visitor was Samuel de Champlain, another Frenchman. De Champlain was sent by French king Henri IV to control the fur trade in the area. In 1608, de Champlain set up a trading post which later became the city of Quebec. Three years later, he set up another post at Montreal, which would help protect Quebec from attacks by hostile Native groups.

During the first half of the seventeenth century, the Algonquian, along with their allies the Huron, who lived north of the Great Lakes, were at war with the Iroquois. The groups were fighting for control of the fur trade in the St. Lawrence region. By 1640, the Iroquois had pushed the Algonquians out of their riverside lands.

European Explorers

The first European explorer to see the river was the Frenchman Jacques Cartier. In 1534, Cartier found the river on the feast day of St. Lawrence and gave it that saint's name. Cartier was searching for the Northwest Passage—a water route around or through North America to the spice islands

Encouraging Settlers

Montreal soon became the center of the fur trade. Each spring, trappers—called *coureurs du bois*, or "runners of the woods"—set off upstream in canoes. They spent the summers in the *pays en haut*, or "the high country," and returned in the fall with loads of furs.

Quebec became the capital of New France in 1663, ruling over French land from Newfoundland to New Orléans. By 1666, the city's population had risen to 3,500, and by 1700, the city had impressive churches, schools, and government buildings.

To encourage settlers to travel to the St. Lawrence, the French government gave estates of land along the river to noblemen, who could then split the land into lots and sell or rent them to colonists. The estates were long and narrow, so that each fronted the St. Lawrence or one of its

Below: *The Chateau de Frontenac, a hotel in Quebec, built in the late nineteenth century.*

17

WOLFE OF QUEBEC

British general James Wolfe's attack on Quebec in 1759 was one of the great battles of the French and Indian War. His army camped across the wide St. Lawrence from the city, preparing for the attack. Wolfe's scouts found a narrow path leading up the Heights of Abraham, the high bluffs that separate the town from the river. Under the cover of darkness, Wolfe moved 4,800 troops over the river in small boats and led them up the bluffs to line up in front of the city. Wolfe's army captured Quebec in just twenty minutes, although the general himself died during the fighting.

tributaries, because rivers were the only routes through the forests.

Fighting for Control

As the French and British quarreled for various reasons in Europe, their rivalries spilled over into North America, where British colonies dominated the east coast north to the St. Lawrence's south bank. British troops attacked Quebec in 1690 and again in 1711. Even though Britain took Hudson Bay to the north from France in 1713, the St. Lawrence remained a French stronghold. That all changed during the French and Indian War (1754–1763). The French and their Huron allies fought the English and the Iroquois. After many battles, the Treaty of Paris ended the war in 1763 and granted all of New France to

Above: *General Wolfe lies dying surrounded by British soldiers and Native warriors after capturing Quebec from the French.*

the British. The territory around the St. Lawrence River was renamed Canada.

British rule of Canada was briefly threatened during the American Revolution. American patriots planned to attack Montreal and Quebec and persuade the French people who still lived there to join the revolution against the British. After taking Montreal, American forces were defeated at Quebec during a blinding snowstorm on New Year's Eve, 1775. The Americans abandoned their plans, and Canada remained under British control until 1867, when it became independent.

New Arrivals

In the twenty years following the American Revolution, nearly half a million people moved to the St. Lawrence region from the newly formed United States. Most settled in what is today the province of Ontario. These people were loyalists—they supported British rule and did not want to live in the United States. Most loyalists were British, although African Americans, Native people, and other European colonists also made the move. Modern Canadians related to these people sometimes use the initials

Below: *A couple look out over Quebec's busy port on the St. Lawrence River in 1859.*

19

BETWEEN TWO NATIONS

The small Mohawk Akwesasne Reserve straddles the St. Lawrence River in the International Rapids region. South of the river, the reservation is within the state of New York; to the north, it is part of the Canadian provinces of Quebec and Ontario. The reserve was established in the 1760s and today is home to thirteen thousand Mohawk people.

The reservation's position brings it under the control of two countries, two provinces, one state, and two Native councils.

During the Vietnam War in the 1960s, Mohawk men living in the U.S. side of the reservation could be called into the U.S. military, while those in the Canadian section could not. At the time, there were stories of some U.S. Mohawks crossing the St. Lawrence River to escape participating in the unpopular war. A few Canadian Mohawks, however, crossed the other way, so they could join the U.S. military.

U.E. (which stands for "unity of the empire") after their surnames.

In 1791, the British divided Canada into Upper Canada, which is Ontario today, and Lower Canada, or Quebec. The two areas developed different traditions. In Upper Canada, British laws and traditions continued, while Quebec was proudly French. French is the official language in the province.

Throughout the late eighteenth and nineteenth centuries, the St. Lawrence was the main highway into

Above: *A Mohawk man living in the St. Lawrence area in front of traditional summer shelters.*

inland Canada. By 1830, about thirty thousand new arrivals were passing through Quebec each year. Early in the twentieth century, the annual totals were more than one hundred thousand, but then World War I (1914–1917) reduced the number of new immigrants.

The river was also the basis of Canada's early industry, as the technology of Europe's Industrial Revolution was brought over to North America. Industrialization meant that iron foundries and mining became big businesses in the region, rivaling forestry and farming.

THE DEADLY ISLAND

During the 1830s, there were outbreaks of cholera, a deadly disease, across Europe. To stop immigrants from bringing the disease to Canada, the government created a quarantine station on Grosse Ile, a small island in the St. Lawrence River about 30 miles (48 km) upstream from the city of Quebec. Immigrants were held on the island while doctors checked them for cholera.

The island soon became overcrowded and unhealthy. While they waited for their checkups, many healthy people caught diseases from other immigrants on the island. The situation became especially bad during 1847 and 1848, when more than 100,000 Irish immigrants arrived on Grosse Ile, escaping from a famine in Ireland. The quarantine station became so overcrowded that 7,480 people died from disease there.

In the 1860s, European doctors discovered that cholera and other diseases were spread by dirty drinking water and bad sanitation. New facilities were built on Grosse Ile and sick immigrants were kept separate from healthy arrivals. By the twentieth century, the island station was unnecessary because immigrants were healthier and infectious diseases were better understood. It closed in 1937.

Below: *A memorial to those who died on Grosse Ile.*

Above: *A road sign in Quebec uses both English and French. The bilingual signs reflect the province's complex history.*

4 Logs, Locks, and Lakes

The St. Lawrence River has been vital to the Canadian economy for a long time. As well as being a busy shipping highway, the river valley is the most populated area of eastern Canada.

Although the St. Lawrence cuts a long way into the interior of North America, it was not always possible for large cargo ships to travel along its entire length. Until the eighteenth century, Montreal was as far as most boats could go. Beyond this point, several dangerous rapids, such as Lachine, near Montreal, blocked the path of travelers. The slower waters of the river were also often blocked with thick layers of ice in winter.

Above: *Paper is put onto huge rolls in a paper mill. The paper is made from trees that grow north of the St. Lawrence River.*

BUILDING THE SEAWAY

Early in the twentieth century, Canada and the United States decided to make the St. Lawrence River easier for large ships to travel on. They came up with the St. Lawrence Seaway, a series of projects between Montreal and Lake Ontario that would link the river by way of the Great Lakes to ports as far away as Duluth, Minnesota, 2,340 miles (3,765 km) from where the St. Lawrence meets the Atlantic Ocean.

Construction began in 1954, and it took about 22,000 workers five years to complete the work. The river's channel was widened and deepened in several places, and 65 miles (105 km) of canals, three dams, and fifteen locks were built. The concrete for the seaway was enough to build a 1000-mile- (1600-km-) long highway. About 6,500 people had to be relocated from their homes to make way for the waterway.

The seaway was jointly built by Canada and the United States. Both countries would gain from increased traffic on the river. Although ships pay tolls to use the seaway, it has yet to pay for itself.

Changing the River

The first canal around the Lachine rapids was dug by French monks in 1700. Over the next 250 years, the St. Lawrence was deepened, diverted, and tamed many more times. In the 1950s, an enormous series of projects created the St. Lawrence Seaway. The seaway is made up of canals, locks, and deepened channels. Combined with canals between each of the Great Lakes, the seaway links the Atlantic Ocean with large Midwest ports, including Cleveland, Ohio, Detroit, Michigan, Chicago, Illinois, and Duluth, Minnesota.

The Midwest and the prairies of central Canada are some of the great grain-growing regions of the world, and grain is the main product carried on the St. Lawrence River. It is brought across the Great Lakes and down the river to Montreal in specially-designed ships called lakers. In terms of modern cargo ships, lakers are small, so they can fit through the many locks in the seaway. The largest lakers are the length of two football fields and half as wide. The shallowest parts of the seaway are only 26.5 feet (8 m) deep. Even the largest

Above: *The construction of the St. Lawrence Seaway was an enormous task, as this 1957 picture of one of the locks being built shows.*

lakers are designed to pass through water this shallow. When the water level in the seaway is low, however, the ships must unload some of their cargo to get through the shallowest stretches.

River Industries

Montreal is the largest grain port in the world. Grain is transferred from the lakers to larger oceangoing vessels at the port. The lakers head back up the river loaded with iron ore, which is the second-most important cargo shipped on the St. Lawrence.

The rocks north of the river are a rich source of minerals. One of the reasons the seaway was constructed was to transport iron ore from the Canadian provinces of Quebec and Labrador to the industrial cities of the Midwest. Coal from U.S. mines, meanwhile, is shipped the other way through the Great Lakes to factories along the river.

Before the river became industrialized during the twentieth century, the main industries were agriculture, the fur trade, and logging. Low-lying agricultural land

Above:
Thousands of logs are floated down a tributary of the St. Lawrence in Ontario, before being turned into paper.

is still used to grow potatoes, vegetables, grain, and hay, while syrup is made from the sap of sugar maple trees.

The logging industry began in the early seventeenth century. It was dangerous work—lumberjacks used hand axes and saws to cut down pines and make the sides of the trees flat. These flattened logs—called "sticks"—were dragged out of the forest by horses to the edge of the river, where hundreds of them were lashed together into long rafts. These rafts were floated to Quebec or Montreal, where they were loaded onto ships bound for Europe. By the early twentieth century, the sticks

KEEPING THE RIVER ICE FREE

Winters are cold in Quebec, and the St. Lawrence River around Montreal often freezes over between December and February. The ice is sometimes 2.5 feet (.76 m) thick. Fishers erect huts on the ice and drill fishing holes down to the water beneath. Farther down the river, in the estuary, thick crusts of ice cling to both shores of the river and loose chunks of ice float in the fast-flowing channel, causing danger to winter shipping vessels.

Because of ice, the St. Lawrence Seaway and the Great Lakes are only navigable for nine months a year. Some locks along the seaway use giant air pumps to churn up the cold water and keep it from freezing solid. It is too expensive to keep all the canals and locks on the entire seaway free of ice throughout the winter, however. The last ships must get through the seaway before the end of the year or risk being stuck in ice until spring. Montreal, however, is the most important port in eastern Canada. Icebreakers—tough ships designed to smash through ice—keep the port's channels clear all year-round, so cargo ships can reach the city from the ocean.

An icebreaker docks beside the wide river estuary. This vessel creates a path through the ice for ships heading upriver.

PIERRE RADISSON

were cut into planks at riverside sawmills before being loaded onto ships. Wood from the forests of the St. Lawrence River is also used for making paper. Today, papermaking has become one of Quebec's main industries. Most paper mills are located in Trois-Riviéres, the city of Quebec, and Saguenay.

Water power

Many of the fast-running tributaries of the St. Lawrence River have dams built across them, which are used as hydroelectric power plants. The dams harness the river's force to turn giant turbines that generate electricity. The St. Maurice River alone, for example, has eight power plants that

Below: *Coal is loaded onto a laker at Cleveland, Ohio, for transportation through the St. Lawrence Seaway to Canada.*

THE SEAWAY'S WATER STAIRCASE

The Welland Canal allows ships to travel around Niagara Falls, between Lake Ontario and Lake Erie. The 27-mile (43-km) canal system was constructed in 1932 and extends from Port Weller on Lake Ontario to Port Colborne on Lake Erie. It has eight locks, which can pass even the largest lakers. Lake Erie is 327 feet (100 m) higher than Lake Ontario, and the Welland Canal's locks (below) raise and lower ships between the two lakes. It takes eight hours for a ship to move through the canal. The lakers carry 65 million tons (60 million tonnes) of cargo through the canal every year.

together generate more than 1.5 million kilowatts of power—enough to light two million homes. Plants on the Ottawa River supply power for much of eastern Canada.

When the Beauharnois Power Plant was built in 1936 across the St. Lawrence River 30 miles (48 km) downstream from Cornwall, Ontario, it was the largest hydroelectric plant in the world. Today, its thirty-six turbines still generate vast amounts of electricity, some of which is sold to the cities across the border in the United States.

The ready supply of cheap power has attracted industry to the St. Lawrence River region. Although older industries, such as paper production and aluminum extraction, remain important, many newer industries, including plastic and chemical plants, are coming to the region.

5 Places to Visit

The St. Lawrence River and the surrounding area have some incredible sights to see—from the Niagara Falls to the immense Manicougan Crater.

① Niagara Falls, New York and Ontario
One of North America's most visited natural wonders, Niagara Falls is actually two waterfalls straddling the U.S. and Canada border on the Niagara River between Lake Ontario and Lake Erie.

② Lake Ontario, New York and Ontario
The smallest and deepest of the five Great Lakes. Canada's largest city, Toronto, Ontario, is on the shore of the lake.

③ St. Lawrence Islands National Park, Ontario
Canada's smallest national park contains twenty-one islands in the Thousand Islands section of the river. The nearby Thousand Islands Bridge joins Canada and the United States. The 8.5 mile (14 km) bridge actually includes three bridges linking islands in the river.

④ Montreal, Quebec
Montreal was founded by French settlers on a 31-mile- (50-km-) long island in the St. Lawrence in 1642. Nearly three-quarters of the population still speak French. Montreal has a remarkable underground city, full of malls, movie theaters, and restaurants where city residents are protected from the bitterly cold winter weather.

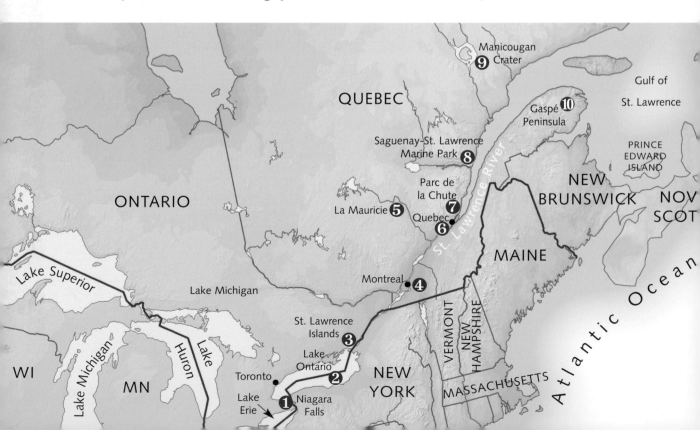

4 *One of the underground malls in Montreal.*

⑤ La Mauricie National Park, Quebec

Most of La Mauricie is covered by a wilderness of forested hills and valleys, with many lakes and peat bogs. For more than eight thousand years, the area was home to the nomadic Attikamela people.

⑥ Old Quebec, Quebec

Founded in 1608, Quebec is the oldest city in Canada. The city has two historic sections: Vieux Port (the "old harbor") on the bank of the river and the Haute Ville ("upper town"), which stands on the 300-foot (90-m) cliffs above the river.

⑧ Saguenay-St. Lawrence Marine Park, Quebec

In 1990, this park was established to protect more than 386 square miles (1,000 sq km) of water and land around the junction of the Saguenay and St. Lawrence Rivers. It includes the spectacular Saguenay Fjord, where cliffs rise to over 1,300 feet (400 m).

⑨ Manicougan Crater

This giant meteorite crater is filled with the largest artificial lake in North America—the sixth largest in the world. The lake was created when a dam was built across the Manicougan River—a branch of the St. Lawrence—in 1968. The large island in the middle of the lake was produced by the meteorite's impact.

⑩ Gaspé Peninsula

Gaspé Peninsula is a remote region on the south side of the St. Lawrence near the river's mouth. The area is popular with bird-watchers, who come to see the many migrating birds that visit the area.

⑦ Parc de la Chute, Quebec

The highlight of this park is a beautiful waterfall that tumbles 272 feet (83 m) into the St. Lawrence, making it more than 100 feet (30 m) taller than Niagara Falls. In winter, the spray forms a mound of ice at the bottom of the falls. It is a favorite pastime to slide down the ice mound, while braver people (right) climb the frozen falls.

How Rivers Form

Rivers have many features that are constantly changing in shape. The illustration below shows how these features are created.

Rivers flow from mountains to oceans, receiving water from rain, melting snow, and underground springs. Rivers collect their water from an area called the river basin. High mountain ridges form the divides between river basins.

Tributaries join the main river at places called confluences. Rivers flow down steep mountain slopes quickly but slow as they near the ocean and gather more water. Slow rivers have many meanders (wide turns) and often change course.

Near the mouth, levees (piles of mud) build up on the banks. The levees stop water from draining into the river, creating areas of swamp.

❶ **Glacier:** An ice mass that melts into river water.

❷ **Lake:** The source of many rivers; may be fed by springs or precipitation.

❸ **Rapids:** Shallow water that flows quickly.

❹ **Waterfall:** Formed when a river wears away softer rock, making a step in the riverbed.

❺ **Canyon:** Formed when a river cuts a channel through rock.

❻ **Floodplain:** A place where rivers often flood flat areas, depositing mud.

❼ **Oxbow lake:** River bend cut off when a river changes course, leaving water behind.

❽ **Estuary:** River mouth where river and ocean water mix together.

❾ **Delta:** Triangular river mouth created when mud islands form, splitting the flow into several channels called distributaries.

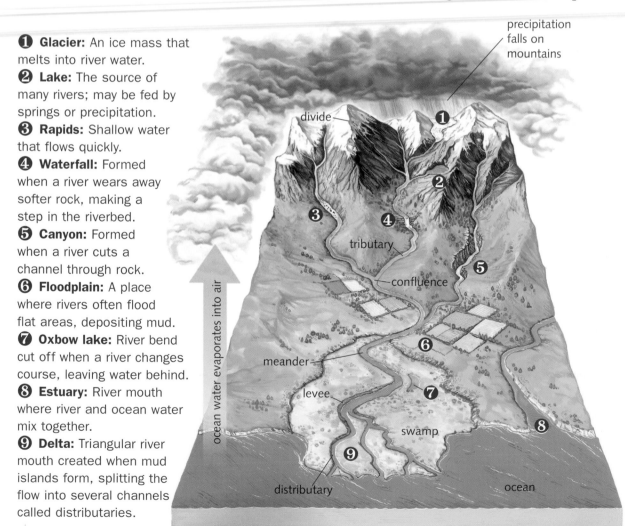

precipitation falls on mountains

divide

tributary

confluence

meander

levee

swamp

distributary

ocean

ocean water evaporates into air

Glossary

barge A flat-bottomed boat used to transport goods and usually pulled or pushed by a tug.

basin The area drained by a river and its tributaries.

canal A man-made waterway used for navigation or irrigation.

cargo Transported products or merchandise.

confederacy People united in a league to support common interests.

confluence The place where rivers meet.

dam A constructed barrier across a river that controls the flow of water.

dock A place where ships load and unload.

freshwater Inland water that is not salty.

gorge A narrow, steep sided valley or canyon.

harbor A sheltered area of water deep enough for ships to anchor.

Immigrant A person who moves to another country from his or her native land.

lock A section of a river that is enclosed by gates. The level of water inside the lock can be raised or lowered so boats can travel between stretches of water that are at different levels.

navigate To travel through water, steering in an attempt to avoid obstacles.

ore Stone that contains metal or other valuable elements.

rapids Shallow parts of a river where the water runs very fast.

saltwater Seawater or other bodies of water that are salty.

tidal Rising and falling water levels that occur because of tides.

tributary A river that flows into a larger river at a confluence.

valley A hollow channel cut by a river, usually between ranges of hills or mountains.

waterway A river or canal that boats can travel on.

For Further Information

Books

Armbruster, Ann. *St. Lawrence Seaway.* Children's Press, 1997.

Fischer, George. *Sentinels in the Stream: Lighthouses of the St. Lawrence River.* Boston Mills Press, 2001.

Gibbons, Gail. *The Great St. Lawrence Seaway.* William Morrow and Company, 1992.

Parker, Steve. *Eyewitness: Pond and River.* DK Publishing, 2000.

Web Sites

1000 Islands Virtual Travel Guide www.visit1000islands.com

Great Lakes St. Lawrence Seaway System www.greatlakes-seaway.com

Quebec Tourest Guide www.quebecweb.com/tourism/fleuveang

River Lore www.novatech.on.ca/nautical/riverlore.html

Index